Pastor Russell
Leads the Flock

Pastor Russell

Russell

Leads the Flock

••••••••••••••••••••••••••

Clyde Walker

HORIZON BOOKS
CAMP HILL, PENNSYLVANIA

To Rev. Russ Oleson,
Who **was** Pastor Russell

Horizon Books
3825 Hartzdale Drive
Camp Hill, PA 17011

ISBN: 0-88965-122-1
© 1995 by Clyde Walker

95 96 97 98 99   5 4 3 2 1

FOREWORD

● ●

Young Pastor Timothy had a short, pointed job description—*devote yourself to the public reading of Scripture, to preaching and to teaching* (1 Timothy 4:13). When Paul laid those conditions down, I wonder if he had the vaguest notion how complicated that role would become by the 20th century.

Being a 1990s pastor is heavy-duty stuff. The preaching, teaching and Scripture reading of Timothy's day are only a fraction of what finds its way onto the typical cleric's plate today. Hands-on efficiency in multi-media, public relations, personnel management, worship trends, computers, finances and biblical counseling are now standard expectations. On top of that, as shepherd of his flock, he also must have the capacity to be all things to all people at all times, and to do it with a smile on his face.

"Smile?" you say. "Smile in the face of all that?"

It does seem to be an impossible task. Unless, of course, you have a sense of humor that allows you to stand back and survey the migraine of ministry with the twinkling eye of a man like Clyde Walker.

With almost three decades of ministry under his belt, Clyde has seen it all, and through the magic of cartoons, he helps us take a lighter look at the perils of pulpit and pew. I don't think there is a pastor alive who could miss seeing his failures and foibles portrayed on these pages. And if he can read it cover to cover without at least a twisted grin at the humor of it all, check to see if he has a pulse.

Thank God for the gift of laughter. Thank God for Clyde Walker and Pastor Russell. Without them the pain and punishment of ministry would be destructive. With them, the sky is a little bluer, the flowers a little sweeter and the frustrations a little less irksome.

But I should warn you. You will meet more than Pastor Russell in these pages. You will also meet your pastor, your parishioners, yourself. We're all in there somewhere and not always in the finest form. If you have the courage to take a few gentle jabs at your own expense, read on. I think you'll find the workout invigorating.

George McPeek
Editorial Director

THE PASTOR WE NEED AT FIRST CHURCH MUST BE
DYNAMIC—AGGRESSIVE—A REAL GO-GETTER!

BOY! PASTOR RUSSELL SURE HAS A UNIQUE
APPROACH TO CANDIDATING!

I DIDN'T KNOW THERE WERE SO MANY VARIATIONS ON SPAGHETTI AND MEATBALLS.

NEXT YEAR, LET'S SCHEDULE THE
SUNDAY SCHOOL PICNIC FOR JULY!

DID YOU KNOW THAT THERE ARE 1,592 PIECES OF
GLASS IN THAT STAINED-GLASS WINDOW?

AT LEAST I SAVED MY SERMON NOTES.

LADIES AND GENTLEMEN, LET ME PRESENT OUR VERY
SPECIAL GUEST SPEAKER FOR THIS MORNING . . .

THERE'S A MUSIC GROUP HERE THAT WOULD LIKE TO SPEAK TO YOU ABOUT A SUNDAY MORNING CONCERT.

NO ONE ELSE SEEMS TO WANT TO JOIN OUR CHURCH BAND!

NO! YOU DIDN'T GET ME OUT OF BED!!!

AREN'T YOU GOING TO PREACH TODAY?

AM I THE ONLY ONE WHO FEELS RUSHED
ON SUNDAYS?

WHAT'S THIS? ANOTHER PREACHER
RUSHING TO SPREAD THE WORD?

WHO IS THIS "HERMAN NOOTICS" HE WAS TALKING ABOUT?

PSST, DEAR! I THINK YOU NEED A BREATH MINT!

If I had known you were going to be good,
I'd have brought my neighbor!

I DON'T CARE WHAT THEY SAY, PASTOR,
I LIKE YOUR SERMONS.

YOU KNOW WHAT YOUR PROBLEM IS? PRIDE! STINKIN' PRIDE!

PASTOR, MEN JUST THINK OF ME AS A PLAYBOY BUNNY!

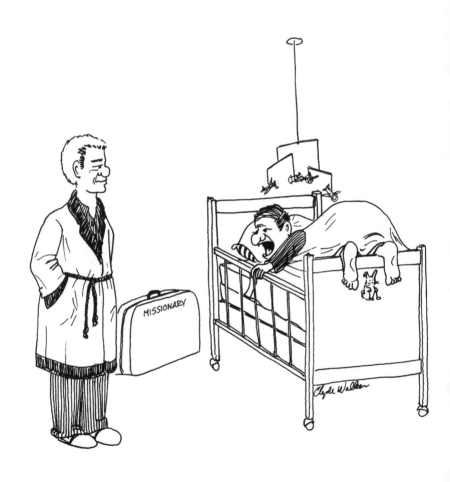

ARE YOU SURE I'M NOT PUTTING YOU OUT?

I'D LIKE TO SHARE WITH YOU JUST A FEW SLIDES
OF MY WORK OVERSEAS . . .

I HOPE YOU HAD A RESTFUL STAY!

PRAYING? YOU MUST BE KIDDING. WRAPPING BANDAGES
IS WHAT REAL MISSIONS IS ALL ABOUT!

LET'S DO SOMETHING DIFFERENT FOR
THE MISSIONS CONFERENCE THIS YEAR.

I DON'T CARE HOW AUTHENTIC YOUR COSTUME IS—
PUT SOME CLOTHES ON!

WHEN I ASKED THE CONGREGATION FOR NEW YEAR'S
RESOLUTIONS, I GUESS THEY MISUNDERSTOOD.

PASTOR, I'VE BEEN OBSERVING YOUR MINISTRY, AND THERE ARE A FEW THINGS I WOULD LIKE TO DISCUSS!

AND WHEN YOU GET BACK, I DON'T WANT TO HEAR
WHAT A GOOD TIME YOU HAD WITHOUT ME!

TODAY'S SERMON HAS BEEN PRERECORDED TO ALLOW ME
TO ATTEND A WEEKEND SPIRITUAL RETREAT.

TAKING INTO CONSIDERATION THE SUMMER SLUMP, FALL
CANNING, WINTER FREEZE AND SPRING FEVER . . .
IT ISN'T ALL THAT BAD!

ANOTHER GOVERNING BOARD MEETING TONIGHT, DEAR?

MR. CHAIRMAN, I DO NOT BELIEVE ONE NEEDS TO
UNDERSTAND THE ISSUES TO SPEAK TO THEM!

AREN'T YOU SUPPOSED TO BE AT THE BUSINESS MEETING?

THE ~~10~~ 11 COMMANDMENTS
1. Thou shalt have no other gods before me.
2. Thou shalt have no idols.
3. Thou shalt not take the name of the Lord thy God in vain.
4. Remember the Sabbath, to keep it holy.
5. Honor your father and mother.
6. Thou shalt not murder.
7. Thou shalt not commit adultery.
8. Thou shalt not steal.
9. Thou shalt not bear false witness.
10. Thou shalt not covet.
11. Thou shalt not Committee.
Clyde Walker

You can wake up now, dear.
The business meeting is over.

THE MESSAGE OF GOD'S REDEEMING LOVE FOR YOU WILL BE INTERJECTED ONLY DURING THE COMMERCIAL BREAKS SO YOU WILL NOT MISS A SINGLE SUPERBOWL PLAY DURING THIS EVENING'S WORSHIP SERVICE.

WELCOME TO OUR ANNUAL DENOMINATIONAL BUSINESS MEETING: THE WORLD SERIES OF RELIGIOUS GATHERINGS, THE SUPERBOWL OF MISSIONARY RALLIES, THE STANLEY CUP OF SPIRITUAL FEEDINGS, THE WIMBLEDON OF THE SOCIAL CALENDAR, THE NEW YORK MARATHON OF BUSINESS MEETINGS THAT GO ON AND ON AND ON AND ON. . . .

HEY—I'D LOVE TO GO TO SUNDAY SCHOOL . . .
BUT SUNDAYS ARE SO BUSY!

NOW THERE'S AN AGGRESSIVE EXTENSION PASTOR!

PARDON ME, SIR, BUT WE'S NOTICED YOU AIN'T BEEN TO
SUNDAY SCHOOL RECENTLY.

THAT'S IT! NEXT TIME I'M GOING TO PRAY
BEFORE I GO CALLING!

IF YOUR PARACHUTE FAILED TO OPEN, DO YOU KNOW
WHERE YOU WOULD SPEND ETERNITY?

DO YOU WANNA CONTRIBUTE TO SPIRITUAL GUIDANCE OF THE NORTHERN ENLIGHTENMENT?

I J-JUST W-WANTED TO INVITE YOU TO THE S-SPECIAL
MEETINGS AT OUR CH-CH-CHURCH!

PASTOR RUSSELL! WAS OUR APPOINTMENT TODAY?

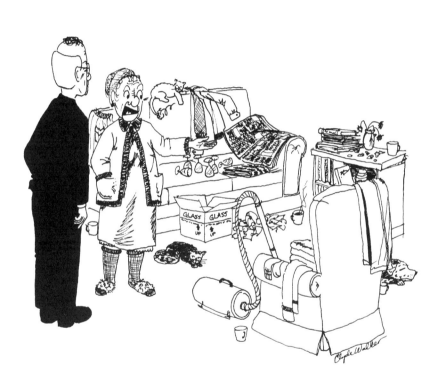

WELCOME, PASTOR! HAVE A SEAT ANYWHERE!

WE GET TO GO TO MCDONALD'S WHEN YOU LEAVE!

NOW KITTY, LET THE PASTOR SIT ON YOUR CHAIR.

SINCE YOU HAVEN'T COME TO SUNDAY SCHOOL,
I THOUGHT I'D BRING SUNDAY SCHOOL TO YOU!!

BAPTISMAL TANK

IT WAS A TERRIFIC IDEA TO BUILD THIS
TO DOUBLE AS A JACUZZI™!

MOMMY! HE'S DROWNING UNCLE CARL!

BAPTISMAL TANK

PLEASE! TRY TO RELAX!

ALL RIGHT, WHO PUT THE FISH IN THE BAPTISMAL TANK?

DID THE BOYS' CLUB JUST HAVE ANOTHER PET NIGHT?

THIS CHART CLEARLY OUTLINES DANIEL'S FOUR APOCALYP-
TIC VISIONS WHICH PREDICT THE COURSE OF WORLD HISTORY.

NO, YOU MAY NOT FEED JOEY TO A WHALE
SO HE CAN FIND OUT HOW JONAH FELT!

I DON'T THINK THIS IS WHAT THE LORD MEANT WHEN HE SAID, "I SOUGHT FOR A MAN TO STAND IN THE GAP."

THE IMPACT OF TRAINED TEACHERS CANNOT
BE FULLY MEASURED!

PASTOR, I DON'T SEE HOW MY FREDDIE COULD POSSIBLY HAVE FLUNKED SUNDAY SCHOOL.

ARE YOU GOING TO TIP ME TODAY OR NOT?

I THINK I'M READY FOR A VISIT TO THE HIGH SCHOOL!

BUT DADDY, ALL I WANT TO DO IS DATE!

APART FROM THE REPULSIVELY CARNAL FORM WHICH IT
HAD TAKEN, THERE IS SOMETHING SUBLIME IN
THE CONTINUANCE AND INTENSITY OF
THE JEWISH EXPECTATION OF THE MESSIAH!

NOW WE CAN MEET THE CHURCH BUDGET!

. . . AND HELP US TO BALANCE OUR BOOKS TONIGHT. AMEN.

MAYBE THIS IS MORE IN YOUR PRICE RANGE.

IF YOU WANT OUR CHURCH GIVING TO INCREASE,
RAISE MY SALARY!

IT'S THE OLD "ASCEND TO HEAVEN JUST
TO PROVE I'M WORTH A RAISE" TRICK.

I GUESS I SHOULDN'T HAVE ANNOUNCED
I WAS SPEAKING ON GIVING!

THIS WEEK ONLY! WITH EVERY $20 CONTRIBUTION, YOU RECEIVE A **FREE** PEANUT BUTTER PARFAIT!

TODAY'S OFFERING FOR OUR "BUILD AS WE PAY"
FUND IS FOR THE ROOF!

THERE'S A GUY IN THE FRONT ROW WHO WANTS TO
KNOW IF YOU LIKE LEMON MERINGUE PIE.

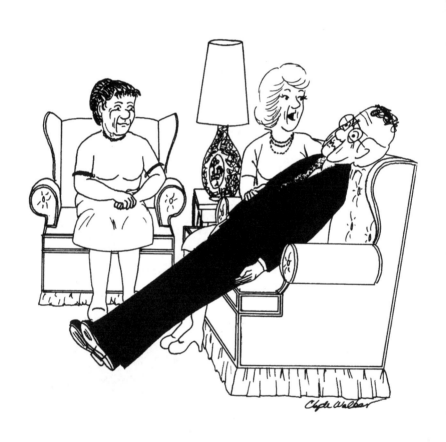

THIS IS ABOUT AS RELAXED AS HE GETS
JUST BEFORE HE PREACHES.

THE POOR DEAR JUST SEEMS TO FALL APART
AFTER HIS LAST SERVICE ON SUNDAY!

CAN WE DEVELOP STAFF RELATIONSHIPS
SOME OTHER WAY?

I THOUGHT HE SAID THERE WAS AN OPENING EXERCISE
IN THIS SUNDAY SCHOOL.

It looks like a bad case of burnout.

LET US STAND AND SING, "LET ME BURN
OUT FOR THEE, O LORD."

DARE I ASK HOW YOUR DAY WAS?

"Pastor, we are real sorry you have hepatitis!
Have you prayed for healing?"
"Do you have sin in your life?"
"I had three acquaintances who died of hepatitis!"

TILL DEATH DO US PART, YOU SAY?

I THINK BABY DEDICATIONS ARE SO BEAUTIFUL!!!!

I CONFESS — I DID IT! I PREACHED THE SAME MESSAGE TWO
WEEKS IN A ROW. I DIDN'T THINK ANYONE WAS LISTENING!